everyday moments

First published 2023

A catalogue record for this book is available from the National Library of New Zealand.

Soft cover ISBN 978-0-473-67300-0
Kindle ISBN 978-0-473-67301-7

Cover design by Amanda Sutcliffe

Design & layout www.yourbooks.co.nz

everyday moments

LISA BUSCOMB

This book is dedicated to my Mum and Dad, the two most loving people who have always shown me that the small things really do become the most memorable moments in life.

WELCOME. I'M SO HAPPY YOU ARE HERE

When you pause for a moment, take a breath and look around, you will discover that the true magic of life is in the everyday moments. It's not the big things, the material possessions, the big achievements. It's the mundane moments. It's the little things. It's those moments that at the time you thought were nothing, but now looking back, you realise were everything. When you reminisce on your life it's the everyday moments that you'll be sharing with your grandchildren and replaying in your mind.

My second book Everyday Moments, is filled with 101 daily reminders on the simple beauty of life, on accepting the now. Words, prose and quotes to remind you that life is magic when you fall in love with the small things. Daily reminders, thoughts to ponder and words to inspire. Turn to any page each day and take what resonates and leave anything that doesn't. Life is beautiful, when you realise that it is all the small everyday moments, that become the most memorable moments.

Lisa x

EVERYDAY MAGIC

Find the magic in the everyday moments. The small things. The things that at times you brush off or move through quickly. Because they seem boring or mundane. They seem so small that they're not worth thinking about, nor remembering. But as time passes and you look back at life, those will be the things that hold the most magic. Those little things will be what you crave more of. Those everyday things will be what warms your heart. This is your reminder to enjoy them today. To look for them, love them, and treasure them. The small things really do become the big things.

MOMENTS

Maybe the most memorable moments you will ever experience are those you never dreamed of. Maybe those moments are the little everyday moments, the mundane, the small things, that seemed too simple. But now, those moments are everything. Etched in your mind and on your heart. Forever. Because the beauty of life isn't always what you expect or plan, it's all the unexpected little moments that come together to create a life that truly matters.

WILD ADVENTURES

Here's to a wild life. A life that is always moving, changing, evolving. A life that is unexpected. A journey that isn't at all what you've planned but so often turns out to be even better than you could imagine. A life of lessons, of adventure, of experiences. Here's to a golden life. A life where dreams come true, where beautiful moments meet you every day, where you smile and exhale with happiness at the beauty of the simplicity. Here's to both a wild and golden life. A journey. A life of contrasts, of ebbs and flows, highs and lows. A life that is so beautiful and so perfect. All in its own way.

What if you loved yourself
a little more today.

LIFE IS GOLDEN

Life is golden when you are truly yourself. When you are courageous, and a little scared. When you are bold, yet vulnerable. When you embrace the imperfections because you know they are what makes you, you. When you trust that good things are coming. When you truly believe that you are deserving. When you know that you are so worthy and so loved. When you know that you are enough and you matter. When you stay unapologetically yourself. Life is beautifully golden when you are simply, you.

At the end of the day
you can rest easy knowing that the true magic is
within you.
You are beautiful in every way.
And all your dreams can come true.

Believe in what you dream about.
Trust that your desires are made for you.
Know that you are worthy.
That your life is beautiful,
because it was made for you.

THE BEAUTY OF YOU

A beautiful life is when you can simply be you. Wild and free. Quiet and homely. Loved by those around you. Laughing and excited. Sharing what's on your heart. Discovering your creativity. Being content in the everyday moments. Staying true to you. And never forgetting that the world needs who you were made to be.

EMBRACE THE SEASON

Embrace the season you are in. Don't look to what's next, or back at the road already travelled. Spend time in this moment. Relish the new. Accept the now. Enjoy the mundane. Fall in love with this chapter. It's okay to feel that you desire something more, but know now is not the time. It's not giving up or ignoring a dream. It's knowing that where you today is perfect, for now. Embrace these days. Accept where you are. And remember there is so much more to come.

IT'S ALL IN THE TIMING

Achieving a dream can take time. So never give up just because it isn't happening fast enough. The only person who has set the timeline is you. Release it. Maybe you need to grow a little more before the dream becomes a reality. Maybe the person who will support you with your dream isn't ready yet. Maybe something incredible needs to happen first that will steer you down a slightly different path. Maybe you think this is your dream because society says so, not because you truly want it. Achieving a dream can take time. If it takes time, you are not less worthy nor is the celebration any less rewarding.

BE KINDER TO YOURSELF

Don't be so hard on yourself. Some days, you wake and all the things you want to do just don't happen. You scroll social media when you really hoped to journal. You lay in bed instead of getting outside. You planned a healthy breakfast but reached for coffee first. Your sheets need a wash, and so does your hair. You remember you didn't return your mum's call and the library books are due back. Some days things just don't go to plan, you feel behind and a little lost. But it's okay. Everyone has these days. Take a breath, write yourself a love note, sit and enjoy that coffee, and the slow morning. You probably need the rest. And then remember that every moment is a new moment. And every day is a new day. And then make a change, get back on track, reset. This morning may not have been what you hoped for, but it was exactly what you needed.

Tomorrow is a new day.
Every day may not be the very best,
but every day
is a part of your story.

EVERYTHING WITHIN YOU

I hope you know that you are worthy. That you are enough. That you have everything within you to create the person you dream to be. That you are magic, and you can unapologetically follow your dreams. Lift yourself up, be your biggest cheerleader. Invest in yourself, spend time doing what lights you up. Create the story that you see in your dreams. Be grateful for who you are and everything you have. Embrace this current moment. Embrace your imperfections. And be excited for what's next. Know that great things are coming and you are deserving of every one of them.

SAY YES

Don't wait until everything is perfect to say yes, to make that change and take the leap. Sometimes you have to move forward even when you don't feel ready. When you're a mix of nervousness and excitement. That's a good time to take that step. You feel like you need to be a certain someone to say yes and follow your heart, but who you are today is exactly who you need to be.

FEELING CREATIVE

And one day, you discovered that creativity doesn't have to be perfect, or big, or out in the world for everyone to see. Your creativity is for you. You don't have to write a book to be a writer. You don't have to sell art to be an artist. You don't have to have a clothing label to sew. You don't have to share your creations with anyone to be a creative. If you have a creative passion, you are a creative. Give yourself permission to live a creative life.

TODAY, LET YOURSELF JUST BE

Allow yourself the time to just be today. Love, laugh, play, create and rest. Discover the magic in the simple things. Don't make plans, allow the space of the day. Embrace the moments that you've missed. Meet with a friend and talk. Take a walk. Eat what your heart desires. Start that book or art project that you've been waiting on. Pj's all day. Indulge in the most beautiful self-care. Find the space to just be. Find the magic in being free. To enjoy. To fill your cup. And remind yourself that sometimes the slow days are the very best days.

And on those days that you don't feel worthy,
please know that someone is inspired by all that you are.

A LITTLE MORE

I've decided that every day I will be a little more me. I will do a little bit more of what I love and a little less of what I think I should be doing. I will look in the mirror and like what I see a little bit more. I will feel a little prouder of everything I have achieved and the journey I have travelled. I will feel a little more grateful for all that I have in my life. I will focus a little more on the things I can control and leave aside the things that are out of my control. Every day I will be a little more me.

THE GREATNESS WITHIN

It can be so easy to look at others and see their beauty and amazing qualities. It can be so easy to see others greatness. But the greatness you see in others is also inside of you. And while you are watching others, they are watching you; inspired, proud and excited for all you are and all that is to come.

BEING YOU

You don't need to be the best in the game. You don't need to be like them. You don't need to do it the way they do it. Because what if I told you that the way they do it wouldn't work for you anyway. We are all unique and bring our own magic to this world. Your uniqueness is your superpower. What you find weird about yourself, is what other people love. Your quirks are what will make your dreams come true. You have to trust. You have to believe that being unapologetically you is going to create the most beautiful life. You have to honour yourself, fall in love with being you. Don't watch over the fence to what they are doing. Watch the path in front of you. Because that path is going to lead you to some amazing places, better than you could ever imagine.

SOMEONE'S DAY

And on the days that you don't feel worthy, I want you to remember. That you made someone's day today when you smiled their way. Someone right now is thinking of you. Someone is inspired by your talents and creativity. Someone loves you. You make someone's life better.

HIDDEN BEAUTY

It's never too late to fall in love with yourself. To discover the parts that make you unapologetically you. To find the hidden beauty that is within. To discover those parts that others have always admired, but you are only now seeing. Shine your light. Be brave. Be open. Be yourself. Fall in love with yourself. Because the world needs the magic only you can bring.

The greatness you see in others is also inside of you.
And while you are watching them,
they are watching you; inspired, proud and excited.

THOUGHTS ON LIVING

Never forget that there are goals, and there is life. And the two sometimes don't intertwine. It can be easy to get lost in your goals, in looking forward, in achieving, in dreaming of the next milestone. And this is not a bad thing. It's important, and motivating and exciting. But while you are striving forward, don't forget to pause every now and then, and enjoy life. Enjoy the moments in between, the now. Because whilst where you are heading looks good, right now looks good too.

And on the hard days I want you to remember this.
You are amazing. You are beautiful inside and out.
You are courageous, brave and you do hard things.
You are inspiring. You are loved.
You are so worthy. You matter.

Someone right now is so happy
you are in their world.

STAY GOLDEN

Here's to golden sunsets, cool water swims and long slow chats. Here's to drinks with friends, cuddles with loved ones and falling in love with yourself. Your life is yours to live. Embrace it, fall in love with it, do the things that light you up. And then do more of them. Here's to living in the moment. In this moment, because really that is all we have. Here's to discovering all the beauty that is right in front of you. Here's to living the life that you dream of.

Allow every situation to be what it is.
And not what you think it should be.

PERFECTLY IMPERFECT

I hope you know that everything about you is just as it should be. The things you don't like about yourself are what others love most about you. The things you want to change, are the things that make you so beautifully unique. Embrace the imperfections. Embrace the imperfect because those small things, they are the truly magic. And even if you can't see them today. I promise, one day you will. And that day, may not be far away.

WOULD YOU BELIEVE ME

What if I told you everything you dreamed of is on its way to you. Would you believe me. Or do you feel unworthy. Do you feel you aren't good enough, that it couldn't be possible. That the dreams you hold in your heart are for others, and not for you. What I want to remind you today is that you are worthy. That you are wildly capable. That those dreams are yours for a reason. That you can achieve everything you dream of. It will happen. Trust it. Believe it.

THE SMALLEST STEP

Never underestimate the power of a small step, a tiny change, one decision. Sometimes it's the smallest step that can lead you to a beautiful new path. Sometimes that first little change can lead to ten big changes. Sometimes that one decision changes everything. You don't need courage to always take the giant leaps, sometimes you just need the courage to take the tiniest step.

JUST BEING YOU

I hope you never forget that you are beautiful, inside and out. That you are amazing. That you make someone's life better just by being you. That you are wholeheartedly worthy. That you are worthy, not because of all that you do, but because of who you are.

It really is the little things
that become the big things.

TODAY'S MANTRA

And one day I decided to do it all for me. To follow what lights me up and listen to my heart. To say yes when it felt good and to say no if I felt that way. To put myself first and fill my own cup. To spend more time with people that brought me joy and less time with people that took it away. To be more me. To know my voice matters. To know I am beautiful. To know I am worthy. To know I matter. And today, I want to give you permission to do it all for you. Because you are worthy, and you matter.

What if everything worked out
even better than you imagined.

ALL OF IT

It's so interesting that the things right in front of you, you once deeply desired. It's interesting that moments in your past that you felt you would never get through, now seem a distant memory. It's so interesting that the days and years are never the same. Life is not about standing still. Life can be unexpected, and it will be unexpected. You will move through challenges and tough times. And you will get through them. Everything you go through, will at one point be in the past. All of it. You will get to the other side. So, if today is a hard day, and you feel like something is never ending. Please know that it will end and you will get to the other side. All of it, will one day, be in your past.

A MOMENT OF QUIET

Some moments you feel like the days are just passing you by. It's mundane. It's slow. Things are hard. Your dreams and desires feel so far away. But what I want to remind you today is that life is always changing; you are always growing and evolving. We live through many seasons. Highs, lows and everything in between. Every season is not the best of times. So maybe this moment is a quiet season, a space to just be. Maybe the challenges right now are preparing you for what's next. Maybe now is a time that seems insignificant, but when you look back, you may see how beautiful it really was. Just not for the reasons you are searching for in this moment.

Keep going.
You are doing better than you think.
Everything is going to be okay in the end.
Keep believing, keep trusting, keep going.

HERE IS GOOD

Right now, things aren't making sense. It's hard to understand why everything has worked out the way it has. But one day, you will look back and feel so grateful for these moments. It may still be painful, it may still hurt, but on that day, you will understand why things happened the way they did. Everything will then make sense. You started a new adventure; you took a new path. It was rocky, and it wasn't easy, but it took you to the exact place you were meant to be. It brought you here. And here is good.

CREATING MEMORIES

I hope you are always creating the memories. Taking in the small moments. Not allowing the little things to pass you by. Because nothing warms a heart more than remembering the favourite everyday little moments, that at the time seemed mundane, but are now everything.

LETTING GO

I'm learning that you find true happiness when you let go of being who you think you should be. When you let go of life being the way you thought it was meant to be. When you let go of all the shoulds. And you accept where you are right now. In this moment. When you embrace who you are, where you are, and where you are going; when you embrace all of it.

UNEXPECTEDLY UNKNOWN

Sometimes life will amaze you, surprise you, frighten you, sadden you. You don't know what life will bring today, tomorrow or next month. And that's okay. Because life will bring you what you need, not always what you want. And that's the magic. The unexpected, the unknown. Because it's often the unexpected paths that turn out to be the greatest. The times where you release control, and take the steps, follow your intuition, even when you don't know where it will lead. The times where you do your best, even when you don't know what to do. When you trust that's it's all going to be okay. When you trust that this is life. Unexpected. Unknown. But so beautiful at the same time.

A LIFE THAT IS YOURS

I believe the most important thing you can do in this life is discover what makes you, you. What lights you up. What brings you joy. What comes easy to you. What challenges you. How do you like to work. How do you love on others. How do you feel most loved. So many questions to answer but the more you know yourself, the more you can create a life you love. Not a life that looks like everyone else's, or a life that you think you should create, but a life that is truly yours.

Know you don't have to have
it all figured out.
Sometimes the very best things
come from the unknown.

MOMENTUM

It's okay for your dreams to change. It's okay for your relationships to change. It's okay if what you love is different to what it used to be. It's okay if nothing looks like it was. We are always evolving, changing and growing. Just like the seasons, the moon, and the flowers. Nothing is created to stand still. Nothing is made to stay the same. Including you.

And one day your dream became your reality.
At first you were surprised
but then you realised it had never been a matter of if,
it was only ever a matter of when.

ON ITS WAY

What if you trusted a little more. What if you let go of the needing to know the how and the when. What if you just let it be. And trusted that everything will all fall into place. How magical would it be if you could exhale and relax, and worry less. Because the truth is, you can. Whatever is meant for you, is on its way to you. Place your energy into loving yourself a little more. Into taking the next step even if you don't know exactly where it will lead. Into being the most unapologetic you. Because when you trust a little more, life becomes a little easier, and a lot more magical.

ENDINGS PART ONE

What if an ending isn't actually the end. What if you looked at it, not as an ending but as a beginning. A chance for a new start, a new opportunity, a new path. You can hold on so tight and struggle to let go, but when you do finally release, by choice, or because you are forced to, you will notice so much all around you. So much that was always there, but just hidden from your view. One of the hardest but most beautiful things you can do, is to let something go. To release, with love. With trust. To know that something good, something better, is not far away. To know that an ending isn't the end, it's is actually a new beginning.

10 SIMPLE THINGS THAT FEEL GOOD

Watching a spectacular sunset
Relaxing into bed with fresh clean sheets
Eating a meal that just tastes really good
Having time to finish that can't-put-down book
Seeing beautiful flowers in the garden
Watching loved ones feel genuinely happy
Waking without an alarm
A long hot shower at the end of a long day
Snuggling on the couch
Walking in nature surrounded by trees and fresh air

SOME DAYS ARE HARD

Some days are just hard. Nothing goes to plan. You are out of milk. The children are fighting. The family is annoyed. It's raining for school drop off. The car is out of fuel. You forgot about that important thing you needed to do. You don't like your outfit. The clients cancel and the orders don't flow. Some days are just hard. But you are not alone. We have all been there and we will all be there, many more times. Life is not always easy, or always smooth. Life can be hard. But on the hard days, know that this too shall pass. Know that in any moment you can do something you love, that makes you smile, no matter how small it is. Give yourself a moment to breathe, to exhale. Give yourself a moment. And know that tomorrow is a new day.

CAPTURING ONLY MOMENTS

Don't let people rush you. Don't let social media rush you. Don't let the thoughts of what you should be doing rush you. You have your own time line and the way your life flows, is perfect. There are no shoulds and no deadlines. You don't have to be married, buy a house, have children or create a business by any age. And the order you do things in, that doesn't matter either. Social media has a way of sharing highlights, the big achievements. It often misses out the failures, the delays, the times when everything falls apart. You feel all of your life. But only capture moments of others. So, know that life isn't a competition. It's not a race. There is no blueprint. There is no one way to live your life. There is only your way, and your life.

MOMENTS

Life gives you want you need. Life gives you lessons, and triumphs. Hard times, the best of times and the most mundane days. So go with the flow. Go with life. Look for the opportunities and the beauty in the small things. Take your time, go slow, enjoy the moment. Look back with heartfelt gratitude. Go forward with excitement and without fear. But most importantly be in this moment. Because at the end of the day, this moment is everything.

TAKE A BREAK

I've been thinking that it's okay to take a break from learning. From growing, from healing, from doing more. From trying to be more. It's okay to just be in the moment. To know that you are okay just the way you are, today. Growth is important. But so is acceptance. So is stillness. And so is being grateful for this moment and where you are right now.

CHASE THAT DREAM

You get to be who you want to be every day. Every dream you have is yours. Everything you want to do is possible. Don't let others tell you that it's not possible. Because it is possible, for you. And that is where the difference lies. It may not be right for them, but if it is in your heart and on your mind, it is right for you. So go chase that dream. Take that first step. Be that person you want to be. Dive right in, you will find your soft landing. Do the things you are dreaming of at this moment. Because when you own it, take action, and embody the person you want to be, there is no other option than for you to become that person. You are so wildly deserving. I hope you can believe in yourself. Incredible things happen when you truly believe.

FAILING

We are all terrified of failing, of not making it happen or it not working out. But the truth is there is no such thing as failing. There is learning, there is evolving and there are lessons. The fear of failing and overthinking can destroy your dreams and happiness. This fear is holding you back from experiencing, from doing: and from achieving. You can never get there if you don't take that first step, if you don't try, if you're not prepared to fail. Failure isn't the opposite of success; failure is a part of the journey. Failures are a stepping stone. Never be afraid of failing. be more afraid of standing still and not trying at all.

I wish you could see what I see you in.
You are beautiful.
You are unique
You are courageous
You are magic.
You are you

SMALL STEPS & GIANT LEAPS

Every dream is achieved with individual small steps. Sometimes there will be giant leaps. Sometimes the small steps will immediately follow the last and sometimes there will be space in-between. As we move towards our dreams our focus should be on feeling good. Life is made up of many seasons. Maybe this season is one of achievement and huge growth for you, so you move quickly and easily towards your destination. Or maybe this is a slower season where you take small steps only when the moment feels good. The road to your dream is always evolving, always changing. And this is okay. This is life. Don't push yourself when you feel resistance, go a little slower. Ride the easy flow when it arises. Your journey to your dream is just as perfectly unique as you are.

A COLLECTION OF BEAUTIFUL EVERYDAY MOMENTS

Finding that perfect parking spot
Thinking about something, and then it happens
Falling into bed at the end of a huge day
The first sip of a perfect coffee
Waking up to a beautiful blue-sky day
Finishing your favourite TV series and discovering a new season
Finding the dress, you have been admiring, is now on sale
Trying a new recipe that works out perfectly
Receiving a love note from your favourite person
Welcome home hugs

SLOW LIVING

This month I want to remind you that there's magic in solitude. There's beauty in slow. If you're going too fast, you miss the moment. It's so easy to want to rush, to get it all done quickly, to show others your achievements. But stop worrying about them. I want to remind you to slow it all down, fall in love with the quiet times, enjoy the alone times. Being alone isn't lonely; it's growth, it's necessary; it's where you can really listen. Look for magic in the quiet moments, in the slowness, in the simple things; and life will always be beautiful.

Here's what I know to be true.
It all comes back to the small things.
Everything.
Don't let the small moments pass you by.

ENDINGS PART TWO

Remember some things have to end for better things to come. If something is ending, let it go. Let it fall away, fall apart, release it. Because when you fill your life with things, especially those things that don't light you up or feel good, you don't allow space for something new to arrive. Release, exhale. Be okay with it ending. Because an ending is also a new beginning.

Things don't always happen immediately.
Sometimes the very best things come from
seeds you planted a long time ago.

REFLECTIONS

You couldn't see it at the time. The obstacles, the challenges, the roadblocks had you feeling overwhelmed, fearful and afraid. But now, looking back, it all makes sense. Everything has worked out so beautifully, in its own way. In the midst of the storm, it was so dark. It was a struggle. It was challenging. But you kept going. You pushed through, and you carried on even when you felt you couldn't take another step. And now there is the lightness. Feel proud of your courage, of your determination and your strength. It was only you, who has brought you to this moment. And now everything is coming together. Finally. Slowly. So always remember, you can do incredible things. You have done incredible things. You are incredible.

THERE ARE ONLY CHOICES

Your life is yours to live. You can choose your dreams. Choose your happiness. Choose your actions. Choose your days. Nothing is given. Nothing is set in stone. There are no must-do's. There are only your choices. So, make the choices that bring a smile to your face. The choices that warm your heart. That feed your soul, that excite you. I hope you choose to listen to yourself. I hope you learn to live your life just as you dream to. I hope you live on your terms and I hope you do this each and every day.

ALL THE DAYS IN BETWEEN

Not every day is perfect. It was never meant to be. Every day is to be lived. To be an experience. The good days, the bad days, the best days, the hardest days; and all the days in between. Every day will bring you something. And, all that you need to do, is be yourself, and to do your best. To dream, to take action, to love, to experience, to keep going and look for the magic in every day. Without expectations, without looking for perfection.

A LIST OF WONDERFUL MOMENTS

An airport welcome home hug
A hot cup of tea by your bed when you wake
An 'are you home safe' text
Not being able to put down a great book
Talking long into the night
Laughing and dancing around the kitchen
Pancakes for dinner
Snuggled close by a fire
A compliment in an unexpected moment
All green traffic lights

This moment
is preparing you
for something amazing
that hasn't happened yet.

A GENTLE REMINDER

This is what I want to share with you today. You are beautiful inside and out. You are doing the best you can with where you are at this moment. You are smart, courageous, and brave. There are people who love you so much that you make their day better just by being you. Everything you dream of can be yours. You will find more joy when you focus on the small things. You are worthy, amazing, and loved. Someone is dreaming of you right now. There is always light after dark. You are deserving of good things. Please read this as many times as you need to today. I wrote this for you.

EVERYTHING IS FALLING

I know you don't feel like you have made it yet. That you aren't where you want to be. But I want to remind you that where you are right now is perfect. Everything is falling into place and happening in a perfect way. It may not feel like it, but trust, it's all going to be okay. Exhale, breathe, relax your shoulders. The road you have travelled to here has not been easy, but life isn't a smooth path. Life is rocky and bumpy. But where you have been, has brought you here. And the same road will take you exactly where you want to go, or somewhere even better than you could ever imagine. So, trust, breathe out, know that everything is falling into place and happening in the most perfect way.

HERES TO WINTER

Here's to winter. To slow mornings. To duvet snuggles and blanket cuddles. To hot cacao and slow-cooked meals. To fresh blooms, green grass and dancing leaves. To Sunday mornings and cosy nights, fresh sheets and fluffy slippers. Here's to slow tunes, dancing with friends and family board game nights. To the beauty of nature, the changing of seasons, to knowing we are all different yet the same. Here's to full tummies, cosy outfits and self-respect. Here's to Winter.

FALL FEELS

Taking a step towards a dream.Compassion for
myself
and where I am in this moment.
Cooler days and falling leaves.
Hot drinks, warm blankets,
cosy candles and good books.
Self-loving.
Taking it all in.
Being in the moment
and enjoying the magic in the quiet times.

HERE'S TO YOU

Here's to knowing you are worthy. Here's to knowing this is just the beginning. Here's to knowing so much more is to come for you. If you are not yet where you want to be, here's to knowing you are on the way. Here's to knowing that you are doing your best. Here's to being you, unapologetically you. Here's to sharing your voice, your passions, and desires. Here's to being more you and ending each day with a grateful heart. Here's to knowing you are wildly deserving.

IT'S SCARY BEFORE IT'S EASY

Your life doesn't have to be exactly how it looks today. You have everything within you to make a change. Change your thoughts, change your routines, change your habits. Make a change, any change. A small step or a giant leap. Dip your toe in or take the jump. There is something new in front of you. Trust me If the life you dream of looks a little different to how it is today, make a small change. It's all up to you.

SUCCESS IS A FEELING

Success is so often described as the achievement, but what if success was more of a feeling. What if a successful relationship wasn't one that lasted sixty years, but one that was really beautiful while it lasted, even if only a few years. What if a successful career wasn't one that made you a millionaire or a famous name, but one where you were excited to get started every morning. What if a successful day wasn't one where you achieved a lot but one that was slow and soul-nourishing; where you felt content and, simply, happy. Success is thought of as a destination but maybe we should rewrite it to be a feeling.

INSPIRED BY POSSIBILITIES

You see someone living the life that you dream of. The home, the career, the relationship, the lifestyle. The first emotion you feel may be jealousy. But what if you moved aside the jealousy and instead felt inspired. Inspired by the possibilities. Inspired by the opportunities. Inspired that what you dream of is possible. It's real. And it's achievable. Because the truth is, if they can do it, so can you. Everything you dream of is waiting for you. It's simply waiting for you to believe that it's possible.

DAY ONE

If you're afraid of starting because someone else is already doing it, remember they too started at day one. They too started as a beginner, without knowing a lot, scared. But they started, they gave it a go, they pushed through; and look where they are today. Remember you too can succeed from starting new. And the truth is, you are not starting from nothing. All the years of learning, of growth, of challenges, have given you beautiful experience. And you will use this experience in your new project. And you can succeed. I believe in you. Do you believe in yourself enough to simply take that first small step?

Don’t worry.
Don’t stop.
Stay on the journey.
When it’s ready to happen, it will happen.

MY HOPES FOR YOU

I hope you find happiness, joy and beauty. I hope you can exhale and rest, even for a moment. I hope you take steps towards that dream that has been on your heart. I hope your eyes sparkle and your soul alights. I hope you move forward intentionally, with purpose and love. I hope you live with excitement, anticipation and wonder. This year I hope you live with happiness and heart. And I hope it's your best year yet.

UPSIDE DOWN

Sometimes life doesn't send you what you want. Sometimes life sends you chaos. Everything is shaken, flipped around, and rearranged. Sometimes it's hard, and it hurts. Sometimes life redirects you onto a new path, a different path, a better path. Although, often, in the moment, that can be hard to see. But trust that everything is going to be okay. It may not feel like it right now, but one day it will. One day the heaviness of now will shift. One day, very soon.

TODAY'S REMINDER

Today, I want you to remember this. All the seemingly little mundane everyday moments always come together to create the big moments. It may not feel like it right now, but one day you will look back, and these days, will be some of your favourite memories.

IT'S ALREADY WITHIN YOU

I've been thinking how the real magic of life is within us. We so often search around for our worth. In our jobs, our relationships, our achievements. But all the love, all the worth and all the magic we need is sitting inside of us. Sometimes near the surface, often buried deep. Waiting to be discovered, to be released, to be celebrated. Even if you don't feel like it in this moment, you are already so worthy. So loved. And you matter. Please never forget how much you truly matter.

THE VERY BEST MEMORIES

I've been thinking about how the best memories don't come from the big moments. The most beautiful, memorable, and heart-warming memories come from the small things. The nights with loved ones around the fire. The reminiscing of where you have been and dreaming about where you are going. The memories are made around the dinner table. The conversations, laughter, and hugs. The very best moments in life are the everyday moments, the simple moments. The moments where you are just you, and those around you are just themselves.

Here's to you
May you be brave, beautiful, calm, inspired, excited, embraced; and loved for all that you are.

BE HERE NOW

I'm not sure who needs to hear this, but here is your daily reminder that you are enough. That you matter. That you are doing a great job. That someone loves you. That you are important. That you deserve to follow your dreams. That what you have to say matters, and someone wants to listen. That you are a really amazing person. And that you deserve happiness, however that looks to you.

IT'S NOT YOURS TO CARRY

I know things feel overwhelming. You're trying to hold yourself up. You are trying to push through. You are carrying a lot of your own thoughts. You are holding so much for others too. But here's what I want you to know. Everything you are carrying isn't for you. It was never yours from the beginning. You took it on but it was never meant for you. This is your permission to let it go. Give yourself space. Give some things back. Give yourself permission to put down some things. Exhale. You don't need to carry it all.

Always be open to new opportunities
and new possibilities;
you just never know
where they will take you.

TAKE THE CHANCES

Every morning you have the opportunity to change your life. To start something new. To end something that no longer feels right. To love your self a little more. To love others more and show more kindness. To say yes or to say no. To take a small step or a giant leap. Life doesn't have to stand still. And the truth is it never will. So why not make the changes you want to see. Take the chances. Each day you have the opportunity to change the path you are on. To move closer to living the life you want to live. Everything you dream of is possible, it's never too late.

IN ITS OWN WAY

The real magic happens when you accept life. All of it. The new, the old, the hard times and the good. We aren't here to be happy every day, we are here to feel all the emotions. We aren't here to stand still, we are here to change, evolve and move. Sometimes the new will be welcomed, other times it will be hard. But please know that life is to be an adventure, an experience. Life is the everyday mundane moments. Life is the journey. And life is accepting that whatever happens, everything that happens, is beautiful, all in its own way.

I WROTE THIS FOR YOU

I wrote this for you today to remind you that right in this moment someone loves you. That someone is inspired by your journey and the path you have travelled. That someone can't wait to hug you and see you again. That someone is thinking of you right now.

ON TIMING

I've been thinking that we are so often in a hurry to reach the destination, to achieve the dream, to make it happen. But here's what I know, good things take time. And sometimes the best things take the longest time. Because you aren't there yet doesn't mean it won't happen or that you are not worthy. Everything will happen in its own perfect time. You only need to trust, to keep going; and to fall in love with the process and the journey you travel along the way. And maybe at the end, you will be so proud and excited for how far you've come, that the outcome becomes a little less important.

ON LOVING YOURSELF

What if you were a little kinder to yourself today. What if the words of love and encouragement you share with others, you shared with yourself. Maybe you could write yourself a love letter, or take yourself on a slow walk, or enjoy a nap, or a delicious bubble bath. I know it all sounds a little crazy but you deserve all the love in the world. And the most important love, is the love you give yourself.

What if today became the best day so far.
It's possible.
Anything can happen.
Always be open to the possibilities and opportunities.
Your life really can change in a moment.

I never regret the past.
Because it taught me everything I know today.
Because it brought me here.
And here is good.

A MANTRA ON LETTING GO

And one day you decide to just relax. To let go, to move with the flow, to stop holding on. There is such happiness in freedom. Life is better when you trust, when you allow it all to unfold. Because the truth is life will fall into place exactly as it's meant to, exactly when it should; regardless of how tight you are holding on.

Where you are in this moment
may not be where you expected,
but life has a beautiful way
of working out.

MAYBE IT'S TIME TO PAUSE

Sometimes you know the dream, the outcome and what you want to achieve, but you don't know the steps to get you there. You rush to get started. You take action but it feels unaligned. You take one step forward, and a few steps back. But what if you waited a little longer before starting. What if you paused, until you really felt into your goal. Maybe take an extra moment to check in with yourself. Once you truly believe in your dream, things will start to beautifully fall into place. The steps will appear right in front of you. It will seem like magic, but everything always falls into place, at the right time.

Today, expect miracles.
Expect good things will happen.
Trust that everything will work out,
just at the perfect moment.

IT'S NEVER TOO LATE

To change your mind. To start again. To begin a new career. To focus on your health. To dream bigger dreams. To say sorry. To find love. To educate yourself. To slow down. To notice the beauty around you. To say I love you. To forgive. To love yourself a little more. To walk away. To make a wish. It's never too late. If you're thirty, sixty or beyond, it's still not too late. It's never too late to discover more about yourself. It's never too late to be more you, than ever before.

FEEL EVERY EMOTION

Life isn't about feeling happy in every moment. Life is about balance. It's about good times and hard times. It's about mundane everyday moments. It's about anticipation and excitement, fear and worries. Life is about the whole spectrum of emotions. Don't beat yourself up trying to feel happy in every moment, that isn't what life is about. Feel every emotion. Live life. Live every feeling. Live in the moment whether you are joyful, sad, angry or blissfully happy. It may not feel like a perfect life. But it is a life of adventure, of experience and of everyday moments, just as it should be.

LESSONS FROM A YEAR

You are worthy. Your path may be different but you are never alone. What you eat matters. Being out in nature helps. Sleep is beneficial and beautiful. Gratitude is everything. Slowness is golden. There is magic in the mundane. Doing nothing is sometimes the best thing to do. It's all been a lot. There is a lot out of your control. There is also a lot you can control. Friends and family are like gold dust. Embracing the uncertainty feels good. You owe it to yourself to chase that dream. The words you read and speak make all the difference. You matter.

Where would you be in a year,
month, or weeks' time
if you took that first step
toward your dream today.

ABOUT LISA

Lisa is a writer, dreamer, multi-passionate creator and mother to two young boys living in Auckland, New Zealand. *Everyday Moments* is her second book.

Connect with Lisa.
www.lisabuscomb.com
@words_by_wilde_road

Printed in Great Britain
by Amazon

49944272R00066